Baby Massage

A Practical Guide

by Sally Lansdale

AuthorHouse™ UK
1663 Liberty Drive
Bloomington, IN 47403 USA
www.authorhouse.co.uk
Phone: 0800.197.4150

Published by AuthorHouse 06/06/2018

ISBN: 978-1-5462-9181-7 (sc)
ISBN: 978-1-5462-9180-0 (e)

Print information available on the last page.

This book is printed on acid-free paper.

authorHOUSE®

Introduction

Over 20 years ago, I had the idea for this manual when I used to massage my own babies. It lay dormant in a suitcase till I rediscovered it when I moved house, and I realised that a book of this kind still didn't exist - so I decided to publish it.

Ashley Montagu was an anthropologist who wrote many books on psychology including *Touching: The Human Significance of the Skin*. His description of research into the early development of babies and how they became as adults made me realise the importance of touch and skin contact to help babies feel more "comfortable in their skins".

If babies have the advantage of being massaged from an early age, imagine the benefits to them and their parents in the future.

❦   ❦   ❦

During pregnancy, babies have been used to surroundings of softness and warmth, naked in a dark, confined space with constant contact with their mother. The "Fourth Trimester" is a relatively new concept of encouraging mothers and fathers to give that safe feeling of closeness that their baby loves.

In some countries, babies are in constant skin contact with their mothers. For example, studies on traditional Inuit communities living in the Canadian Arctic found that mothers carried their babies on their backs with skin to skin contact and then they wrapped themselves in fur to protect them both from the Arctic cold. Similarly, babies in warmer countries are traditionally wrapped together, their bare skin in contact, with the mother's shawl made into a sling.

"Kangaroo Care" is also used, with babies strapped to their parents, and this is particularly useful for premature babies. Throughout India, babies receive much tactile attention from their earliest days. From the age of about one month old, babies are bathed and massaged regularly with various oils. In some ancient cultures, such as those of Mayans and Australian Aborigines, babies heads were even "moulded" by the hands.

People have been massaging their babies for thousands of years in many countries of the World. It is only relatively recently that Western society has realised the benefits of Baby Massage and mothers and fathers have begun to learn this ancient art.

Cutaneous stimulation is important in mammals in all stages of development. Touch is the most developed sense in the newborn baby and mothers are encouraged to have close skin contact immediately after the birth to promote bonding.

In Western society, due to cultural and climatic differences, we may have to make a bit more effort to encourage skin to skin contact, and this is where baby massage can help. There are many studies on baby massage, from the Huffington Post to the Cochrane Review, so do look them up. Surely, though, it would be best to try a few of the simple steps in the next few pages and see if it can work for you and your baby.

I started giving Baby Massage Workshops along the lines of this book when my babies were small too. One of the mothers who came to my workshops said:

"It gave me the confidence to massage my baby. I had always wanted to massage him and somehow this gave me permission to do it - both baby and I really enjoy it."

5

Touch: Mother of the Senses

When you consider that babies have been cradled in their mothers' wombs for nine months, their skin in constant contact with their mothers' bodies, it is not surprising that they need "touch" to thrive.

In research, it has been discovered that touch is the earliest sensory system to become functional in humans, animals and birds alike.

In one study, it was found that early skin stimulation in babies exerts a highly beneficial influence on the immunological system, with important consequences for resistance to infectious and other diseases.

For babies in incubators, bonding with parents is particularly difficult and so the soothing touch of mother and father can help to calm any distress.

Even simple skin to skin contact has a calming effect on a baby.

6

When babies are born they are either placed on their mother's tummy or wrapped snugly in a blanket and both of these are comforting for the baby. Also babies have a "clutch reflex", so if you put your finger in their hand they will instinctively grasp it.

Mothers and fathers instinctively want to cuddle their babies, but when they are first time parents or haven't handled small babies before, they may feel awkward or nervous.

By learning to massage their babies, parents can learn to caress them, encouraging the skin contact that babies love and crave.

This book will give you the confidence to start this process of learning with your baby. Start very gently, massaging one part of the body each day to get used to it, then gradually increase to a full body massage.

1

Reasons for massage

Relaxation

Massage is a useful technique if your baby is having difficulty sleeping. Give your baby a bath and then, making sure that you're in a warm and calm environment, gently massage your baby.

Stimulation

If your baby has colic, constipation or pain from teething, a more stimulating massage is appropriate. This will help to increase the baby's circulation to the tummy or gums (these techniques are shown on pages 14 to 21).

Bonding

In many cultures, skin and body contact form an important part of parenting, with many women working with their babies supported contentedly in slings. The rocking, rhythmical movement that these babies experience can stimulate their motor and intellectual development.

Development of Nerve Pathways

We all have such busy lives with work and other activities. This massage time takes a few minutes out of your daily bustle so that you can give your baby actual eye contact and quality experiences.

In newborn babies, touch stimulates the nervous system, which helps it mature by creating nerve pathways to the brain. Through touch, oxytocin is released in the baby's body. This is the "feel good" hormone and helps the baby to feel loved, nurtured and secure.

Another study found that infants who have their skin stroked regularly cry and fuss less often than those who don't.

9

Massage Oil

It is important to use the finest quality oil on your baby's skin. Vegetable-based oils are best, so look for a pure almond oil (or grape-seed or coconut oil). Otherwise, a specific baby product will do and you might be able to find some with herbal extracts such as camomile or calendula.

Pour a small amount of oil into a little bowl. This means you won't have to keep stopping to open and close the lid of the oil bottle and it will help to prevent spillages.

When you are ready, pull your sleeves up and, dipping your fingers into the bowl, warm the oil by rubbing it in your hands. Baby will soon become accustomed to this sound and will associate it with pleasant feelings.

Important Points

Test your massage skills on
yourself first.
Imagine you are massaging a ripe
plum, so go gently.
Not too lightly -
you don't want to tickle.

Wrap areas of the baby not
being massaged in a small blanket.
Use cotton next to the skin
if baby is sensitive.

If you are worried about accidents,
let your baby wear a nappy (diaper)
until you are ready to massage the
tummy and back areas.

After, the massage relax together,
rest, look at books or sleep.
This helps the process of
bonding too.

11

WARM

Make sure
the room
is warm

Now you are ready to start ...

13

Massage Technique

The amount of pressure, firmness,
direction, duration, intensity, rhythm
and speed are all important.

Babies are able to discriminate
between those who, when holding
them, care for them and
those who don't.

If you want to relax your baby, use a small
amount of pressure and go slowly.
If you want to stimulate the circulation use
slightly firmer pressure and
faster movements.

For a more invigorating massage, when you
don't want your baby to fall asleep
afterwards, use more rapid circular
movements.

14

Hands and Arms

Start with the hands, as babies love clutching people's fingers from a very early age. Sit baby on your knee at first and, without using oil, just gently make circular movements on his palm and back of the hand. Then extend the massage to each finger in turn, and thumb and in between the fingers. Then switch to the other hand.

Then lay baby on his back on a soft towel and, taking some oil from the bowl, warm it in your hands first and start to massage upwards from the palm of the hand up his arm using your thumb on the inside of his arm and your fingers on the outside of the arm.

Legs and Feet

With baby lying on a soft towel or changing mat, start to massage her feet and legs. Using some oil on your hands, cup baby's foot in one hand and massage up her leg with the other hand. The thumb will be on the inside of her leg, with the fingers on the outside.

Then massage the whole of her foot, the toes and in between her toes. Use a firm touch and try not to tickle her. Then repeat on the other foot and leg.

16

Back

Turn baby on to his tummy across your knee with his head lying on your left leg. Starting with the neck, massage downwards and outwards, using your right thumb for the right side of his back. Move gradually down the back avoiding pressing on the spine itself. When you have repeated these movements a few times, turn him to face the other direction and massage the other side of his back with your left hand.

This is a very soothing technique and most babies love it. It can be helpful for babies with chest congestion, as it can help to reduce spasm in the muscles that run alongside the spine.

17

Tummy and Chest

By now, baby will be becoming more relaxed and so you can move on to her chest and tummy area.

With baby on her back, massage across her chest in criss-cross movements. Using your right hand, start at baby's right shoulder and move your hand diagonally across her chest and tummy to her left hip.

18

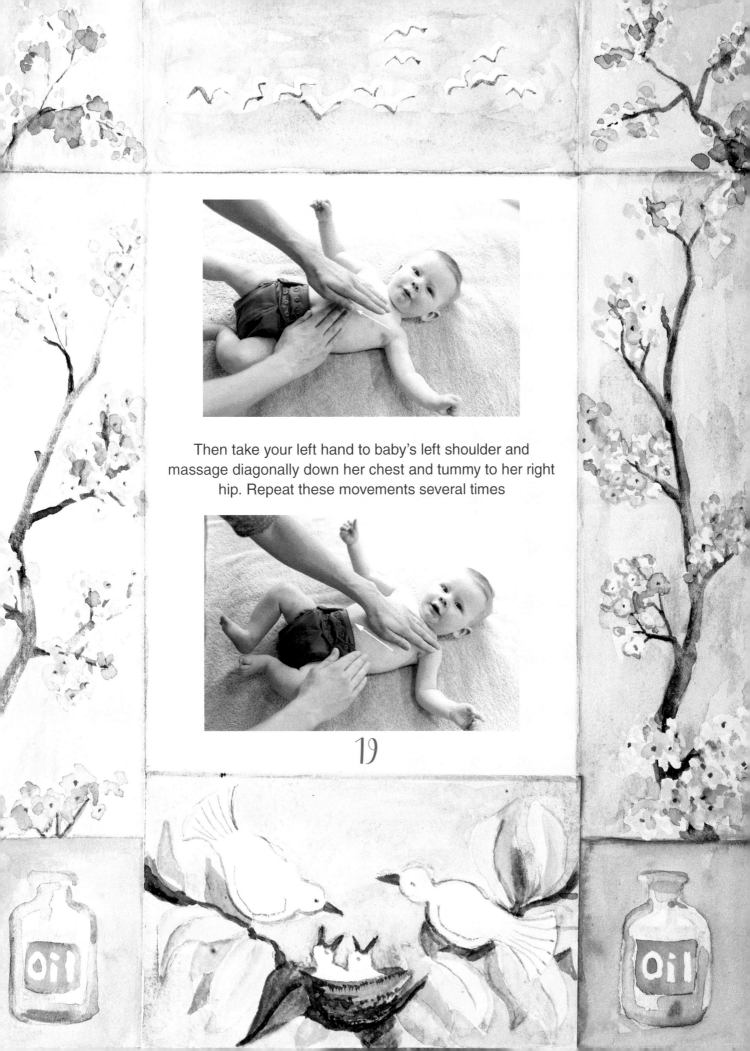

Then take your left hand to baby's left shoulder and massage diagonally down her chest and tummy to her right hip. Repeat these movements several times

19

Head and Face

With baby lying on his back, look at him reassuringly as you massage his face. Wipe your hands so that there is no oil this time. He may be a little hesitant the first time, but once you start to stroke his face, he will begin to enjoy it. Go very gently at first.

Start by using sideways strokes from just above the nose on the forehead. It is easiest to do this from above, so that you don't cover his eyes (as in the photo). Using your thumbs, simply stroke from the centre to the outside of the forehead.

You can now massage his head - small circles as if you were shampooing his hair.

Sinuses and Gums

Now, move so that you can look at baby's face straight on. Place your thumbs on either side of her nose and move them sideways towards the outside of the face. Start just below the corner of her eye and this will help if she is suffering from a cold or blocked sinuses. Move gradually down the face so that you're massaging the cheeks.

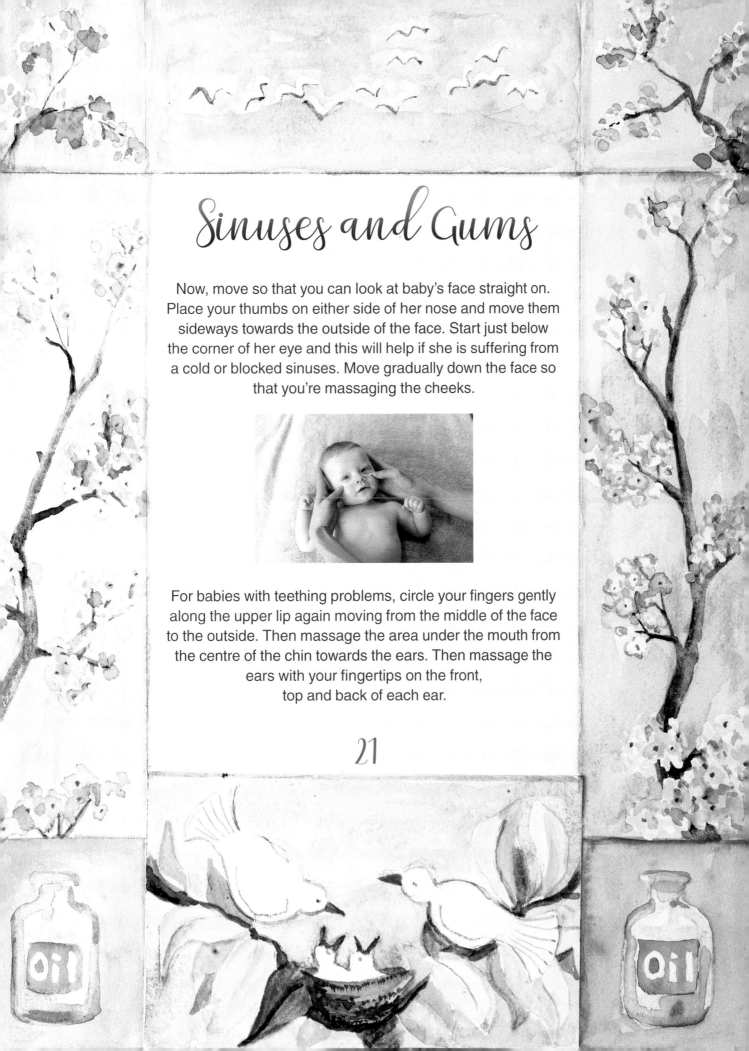

For babies with teething problems, circle your fingers gently along the upper lip again moving from the middle of the face to the outside. Then massage the area under the mouth from the centre of the chin towards the ears. Then massage the ears with your fingertips on the front, top and back of each ear.

21

Questions and Answers

Q   Can I massage my newborn baby?

A   *You can start at any age, the sooner the better, but instead of laying your baby on a changing mat, cradle him in your arms, or lean with your back against a wall, your knees bent and the baby lying on your lap.*

Q   What if my baby wriggles when I massage him?

A   *Your baby may be sensitive or ticklish and unused to this different touch. One way to overcome this is to have the baby in the bath with you and get him used to massage by using a baby soap on him. You can also isolate the area you want to massage and wrap his arms or legs firmly in a towel so that they don't wave around. He will soon become accustomed to the feeling and begin to enjoy it.*

Q   Should I talk or sing to my baby while massaging her?

A   *By all means. She will begin to associate pleasurable feelings with the sound of your voice. If you want to relax the baby, you can talk or sing softly, and if you want to make her laugh, you can make different noises.*

Q   What if my skin is rough?

A   *It's important to look after your hands. When you're changing nappies all the time, you have to wash your hands more frequently, so always keep some hand cream near the wash basin and use it every time you wash your hands. Wear rubber gloves when using detergent or if your water is very hard and protect your hands with gloves in cold weather.*

Q   Can I use aromatherapy oils on my baby?

A   *Unless you are a qualified aromatherapist, it is advisable not to dabble in these potent oils. Stick to pure vegetable-based oils and ones made specifically for babies.*

Q   Can I massage my baby when he is ill?

A   *Always consult your doctor if you are worried about your baby's health.*

Q   What age can I massage my baby to?

A   *It's up to you. If you both enjoy it, you can massage your baby until she's a toddler, or even later.*

22

Acknowledgements and References

A big thank you to:
Beryl Lichtenstein for her lovely illustrations
Seb who was so good while his mother Sarah massaged him
Sebastiano Ragusa for his patience and his lovely photographs
Yousef for his calligraphy and Frances for her proof reading
Ashley Montagu for inspiration from his book, *Touching: The Human Significance of the Skin*, published by Harper Collins (1986)

References:

Barras, C. (2014), *Why Early Humans Reshaped Their Children's Skulls*
Barton, J. (2017), 'The Benefits Of Baby Massage And How To Do It At Home', in *Huffington Post* [Online]
Bennett, C., Underdown, A. & Barlow, J. (2013), 'Massage for Promoting Mental and Physical Health in Infants Under the Age of Six Months', in *Cochrane Review* [Online]
De Boer, R.J. (1969), *The Netsilik Eskimos and the Origin of Human Behaviour*
Gerhardt, S. (2004), *Why Love Matters: How Affection Shapes a Baby's Brain*
Halliday, J.L. (1948), *Psychosocial Medicine: A Study of the Sick Society*
Leboyer, F. (1976), *Loving Hands: The Traditional Indian Art of Baby Massage*
Ockwell-Smith, S. (2012), *The Fourth Trimester: AKA Why Your Newborn Baby is Only Happy in Your Arms* [Online]
Solomon, G.F., Levine, S. & Kraft, J.K. (1968), *Early Experiences and Immunity*

Printed in the United States
By Bookmasters